the dressing up book

lots of ideas for amazing hats, masks, and costumes

By Wendy Baker

Written and Edited by Diane James
Still-Life Photographs by Jon Barnes
Photographs of Children by Fiona Pragoff

A **TWO-CAN** BOOK
published by
Thomson Learning
New York

First published in the United States in 1994 by
Thomson Learning
115 Fifth Avenue
New York, NY 10003

First published in Great Britain in 1990 by
Two-Can Publishing Ltd.

Library of Congress Cataloging-in Publication Data

Baker, Wendy
    The dressing up book/by Wendy Baker; written and edited by
Diane James; still-life photographs by Jon Barnes; photographs of
children by Fiona Pragoff.
        p. cm. – (Activity series)
    "A Two-Can book"
    Includes index
    ISBN: 1-56847-136-X
    1. Costume – Juvenile literature.   2. Handicraft – Juvenile
literature. [1. Costume. 2. Handicraft.] I. James, Diane.
II. Barnes, Jon, ill. III. Pragoff, Fiona, ill. IV. Title.
V. Series.
TT633.B34   1994
646.4'78–dc20   93-21219

Printed in Hong Kong

CONTENTS

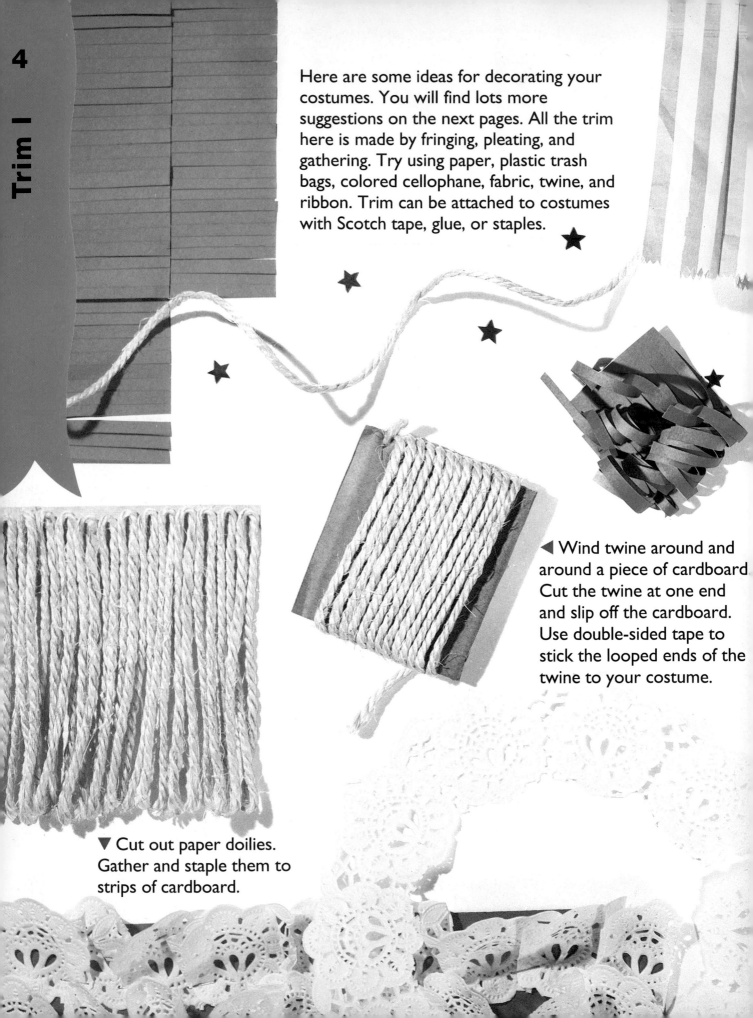

Here are some ideas for decorating your costumes. You will find lots more suggestions on the next pages. All the trim here is made by fringing, pleating, and gathering. Try using paper, plastic trash bags, colored cellophane, fabric, twine, and ribbon. Trim can be attached to costumes with Scotch tape, glue, or staples.

◀ Wind twine around and around a piece of cardboard Cut the twine at one end and slip off the cardboard. Use double-sided tape to stick the looped ends of the twine to your costume.

▼ Cut out paper doilies. Gather and staple them to strips of cardboard.

▼ Cut a square of fabric with a hole in the middle. Make a slit from the middle of one of the sides to the hole. Spread the fabric out and you will have a pointed ruffle like the one below.

Flowers can change an ordinary costume into something really special. Make a bunch and turn them into garlands, headdresses, bouquets, and decorations for buttonholes.

Making Flowers

Cut a strip of fabric, paper, or colored cellophane. Starting at one end, wind up the strip. Secure the end with tape or staples.

You can make different flowers by fringing or cutting triangles in the strip before you wind it up. Another very simple method is to scrunch up facial tissues and secure the ends.

You can also make flowers by cutting out flat shapes and sticking them together like the one in the top corner. Try making leaves in the same way. Score down the center of the leaves and fold gently.

You can make bows from fabric, plastic trash bags, colored cellophane, tissue paper, or crepe paper. Cut a rectangular shape and pinch it together in the middle. Wind a thin strip of the same material around the middle and glue or staple it in place. You can decorate bows by sticking on colored shapes or painting them.

Cut buckle shapes out of cardboard and decorate them with foil, glitter, or beads. You can use buckles for belts or shoes.

Cut two identical circles out of cardboard and make holes in the middle. Put one circle on top of the other. Wind yarn around and around until the hole has almost disappeared. Ask an adult to cut the yarn all around the edge of the circles. Slip a piece of yarn between the two circles and tie a knot before taking the cardboard away. Make tassels by wrapping yarn around a rectangle of cardboard and cutting the yarn at one end. Then tie a piece of yarn around the uncut end of the tassel.

You can save a lot of time by making trim into long strips before attaching it to your costume. You can buy some trim by the yard in department stores. Or, you can make your own by threading flowers, bows, stars, or silver balls (made from crumpled foil) onto yarn, twine, or thread. Make holes in the trim first and thread by hand or with a needle.

Fasteners

You can buy Velcro at fabric stores and at some department stores. It comes in various shapes and sizes, and most kinds have a sticky back like double-sided tape. Tiny fibers on the Velcro cling to each other when you press two pieces together. You can use Velcro to fasten the backs of costumes by sticking down strips or by using button shapes. The Velcro will not show and it is easy to undo when you want to take the costume off.

▶ You can use ribbon tied in a bow to fasten cuffs, necklines, and waists. Keep the ribbon in place with double-sided tape.

▶ Punch holes in fabric and lace together with twine or ribbon. You can use this technique to fasten the backs or fronts of costumes or belts.

▼ Make buckles from thick cardboard. Slot a strip of fabric through the buckle and fasten back one end. Slot the other end of the strip through the buckle and out the other side. If you have any trouble, look at how an existing belt works.

Here are some ideas for decorating paper to use for trim or for a costume itself.

Pleat a sheet of paper and cut patterns in the folds. When you unfold the paper you will have a beautiful lacy effect.

You can print on paper using objects such as sponges, building blocks, or the ends of cardboard tubes. Or, you can make a potato print. Cut a potato in half and cut a pattern on one side. Cover the potato with thick paint and print on the paper.

A very quick way to decorate paper is to dip a thick paintbrush into runny paint and flick it up and down the paper. It is best to do this outside, because it can be very messy.

Many of the costumes in this book need some sort of padding to give them shape. You may want to make a skirt stick out, or to make shoulders look square.

Look out for padding material, such as newspapers, foam rubber, cardboard rolls, and corrugated cardboard.

To pad a skirt, fold a large plastic trash bag in half and staple it at the sides and one end. Fill it with crumpled paper, staple the remaining end, and attach it to the inside of the skirt at the waist. Foam rubber is particularly good for shoulder pads.

It is hard to believe that the beautiful ball gowns here were made from black trash bags! They are decorated with flowers made from strips of colored cellophane. Find out how to make these ball gowns on the next page.

To make the boy's dress shirt, bow tie, and lapels cut shapes from black and white cardboard similar to the ones below. The tabs at the neck of the shirt are used to attach the collar. Cut out a paper doily to decorate the shirt.

You will need about four large plastic trash bags to make a ball gown, and it is easier to make it on the person it is for. Cut the bags open and staple into a long piece for the skirt. Gather the waist and staple as you go along. Double a strip of plastic for the top and pleat and staple into soft folds. Use strips of Velcro to fasten the band at the back. Staple the skirt to the top. Use a wide sash to cover the join.

Decorate your ball gown with cellophane flowers joined together to make a sash.

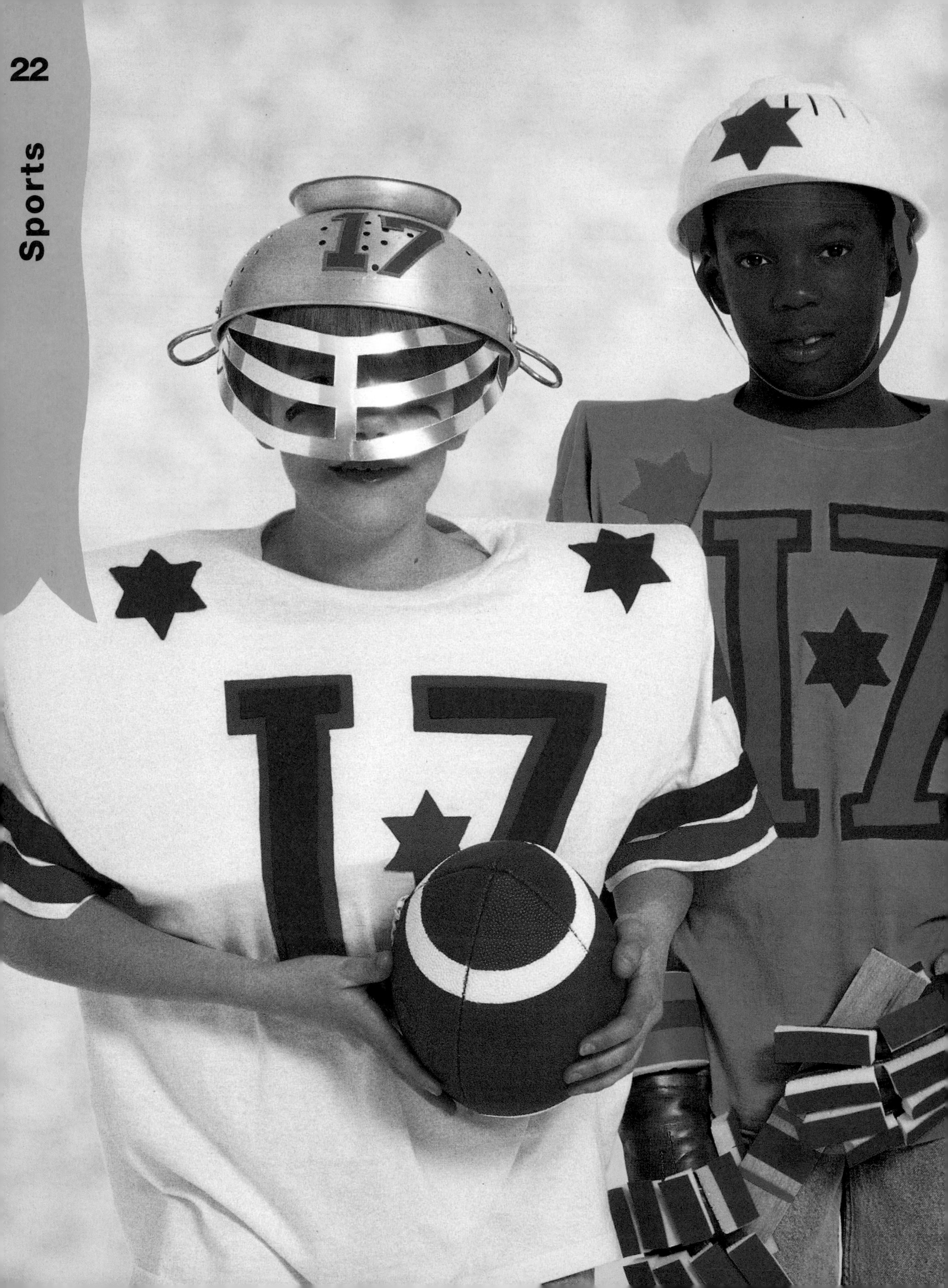
17
17

You do not need to buy expensive sports clothes to look the part! We made our football player's shirt by cutting letters and shapes from felt and gluing them onto a plain T-shirt. The shoulders are padded with pieces of foam. The helmet is a colander with a visor made from cardboard. The hockey player's shirt can be made the same way. For the hockey player's padded gloves, cut pieces of foam rubber – you could use a sponge – and stick them onto an old pair of gloves. Too make our cheerleader's skirt, cut circles out of red and white crepe paper. Gather the waist by pleating and stapling. Stick shapes to the waistband to cover the staples.

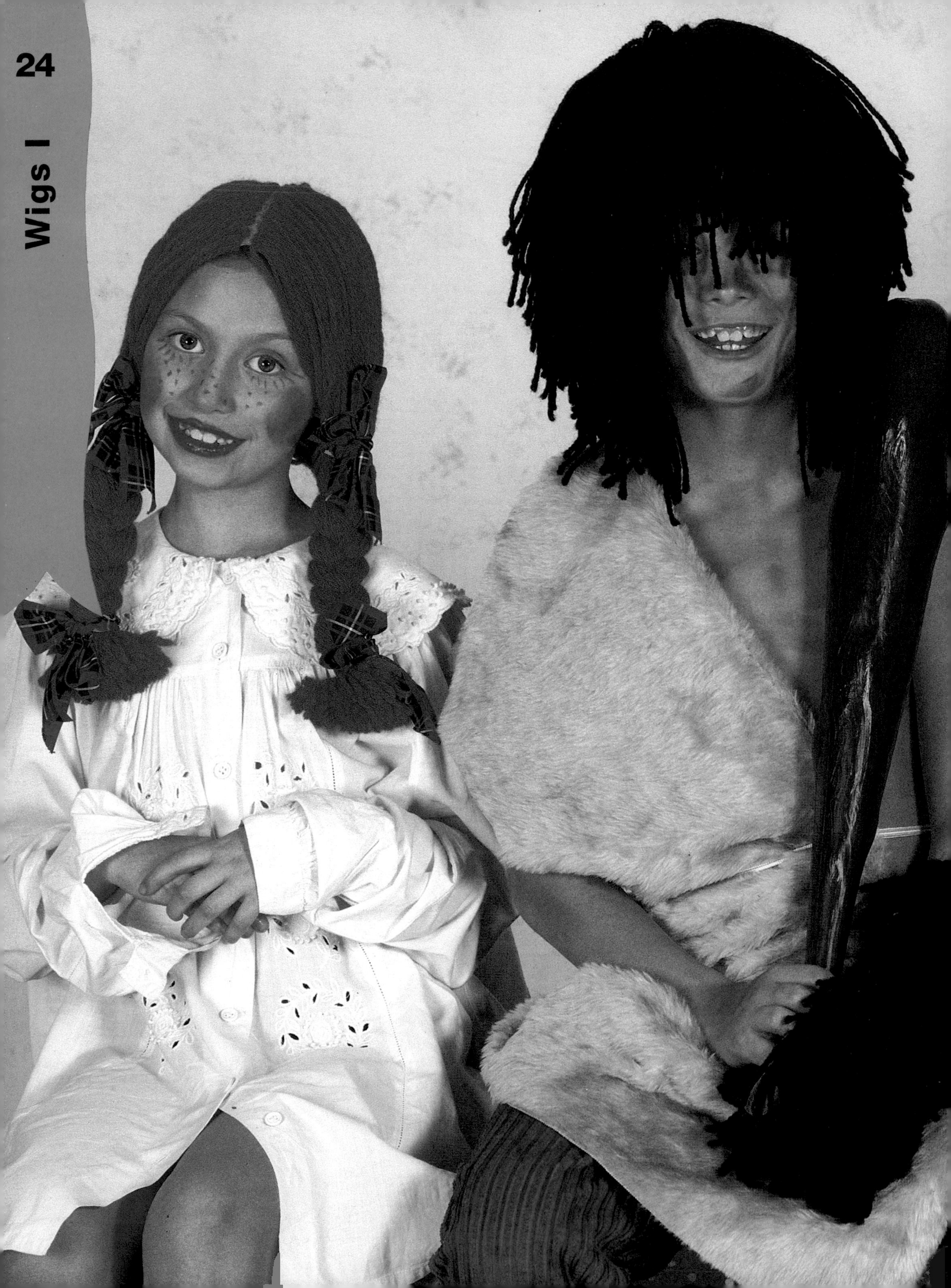

It is amazing how different someone can look with a completely new hairstyle! A wig is easy to make and often adds the perfect finishing touch to a costume.

To make the judge's wig, cover cardboard rolls with white paper. Pierce two holes at the top and bottom and thread twine through. Make one strip of rolls to go over your head lengthwise and attach the side pieces with Scotch tape.

The clown's wig is made by sticking paper curls onto a swimming cap. Make sure the base is completely covered so that it does not show.

Stick long pieces of yarn to a strip of Scotch tape. You can then make braids or ponytails, or you can cut the yarn into uneven pieces to make a shaggy wig.

If you need inspiration for a costume, look at pictures of clothes that were worn in the past. The costumes here are based on clothes that were worn in Elizabethan times in England. Note details such as sleeves, necklines, colors, and fabrics. Make belts, hats, gloves, and jewelry to go with your costume.

We made our Elizabethan costumes from wallpaper with a raised pattern. It looks a lot like the material the original clothes were made from, but is much less expensive. You could also use plain paper and decorate it (see page 14).

First we cut out the main shapes, such as the boy's trousers at the bottom of this page and the girl's bodice and skirt opposite. Try to keep these shapes as simple as possible. Start with a square or rectangle and cut out shapes for the arms, legs, and neck.

We made the lace trim from pleated paper doilies and the beads and buckles from aluminum foil. The boy's ruff was made from two circles of cardboard with a strip of pleated paper sandwiched between them.

It is best to fit the main pieces around the person who is going to wear the costume and then staple or tape them into position.

Elephant Mask

Ask an adult to cut a piece of wire and shape it over your head. Cut ears from cardboard, fold them over the wire, and glue into position. Make a separate trunk from cardboard. Attach string or elastic to the sides and tie around your head.

Bird Mask

Make two holes in a paper plate so you can see out. Glue paper feathers to the plate. Make a beak from stiff paper and glue it onto the plate.

Monster Mask

This monster was made from a clean plastic bottle. Do not use a bottle that contained harmful substances. The nose is the handle of the bottle. Ask an adult to slit the bottle open opposite the handle and make holes to see and to breathe through. Cover the bottle with foil. Pull the slit apart and the mask will grip firmly to your head.

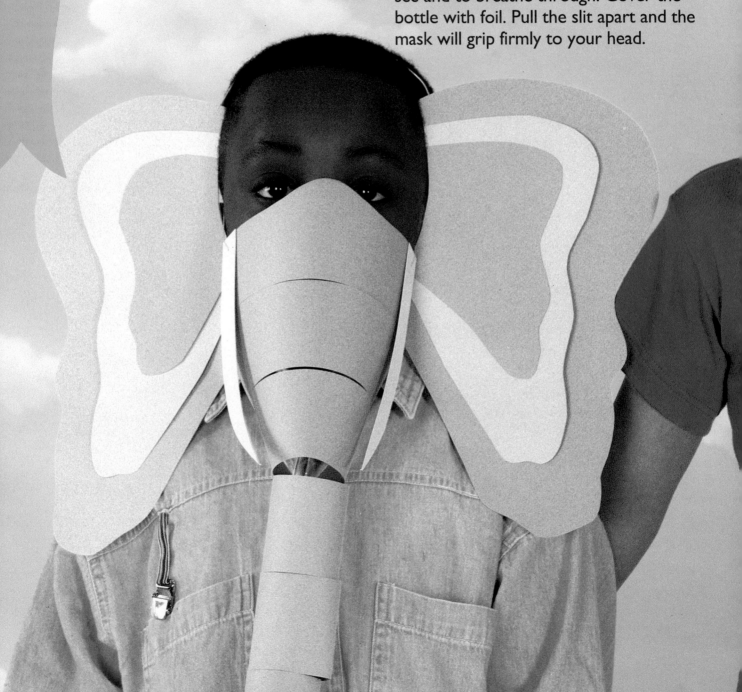

To make the knight in shining armor, we used molded fruit cartons, aluminum foil pie plates, and corrugated and plain cardboard. You can either paint the cardboard silver or cover it with foil. You could use kitchen equipment, such as a colander, to make the helmet.

Our sea monster's costume was made from strips of colored cellophane stapled to a base of clear cellophane. You could also use net or paper strips. The monster's neck and shoulders were made by decorating paper plates stapled to the base. Look at page 32 to see how we made the monster's mask.

If you do not want to hide behind a mask, try making some colorful glasses to go with your costume. Use an old pair of glasses as a guide and cut out cardboard frames and earpieces. Stick on paper shapes, sequins, or glitter. For a finishing touch, glue a sheet of colored cellophane to the back of the glasses. You could also bend a piece of wire to make frames for a more serious pair of glasses.

To make our round present, we used a sheet of thin cardboard rolled into a tube and stapled at the back. The ruffles at the top and the bottom are made from pleated paper.

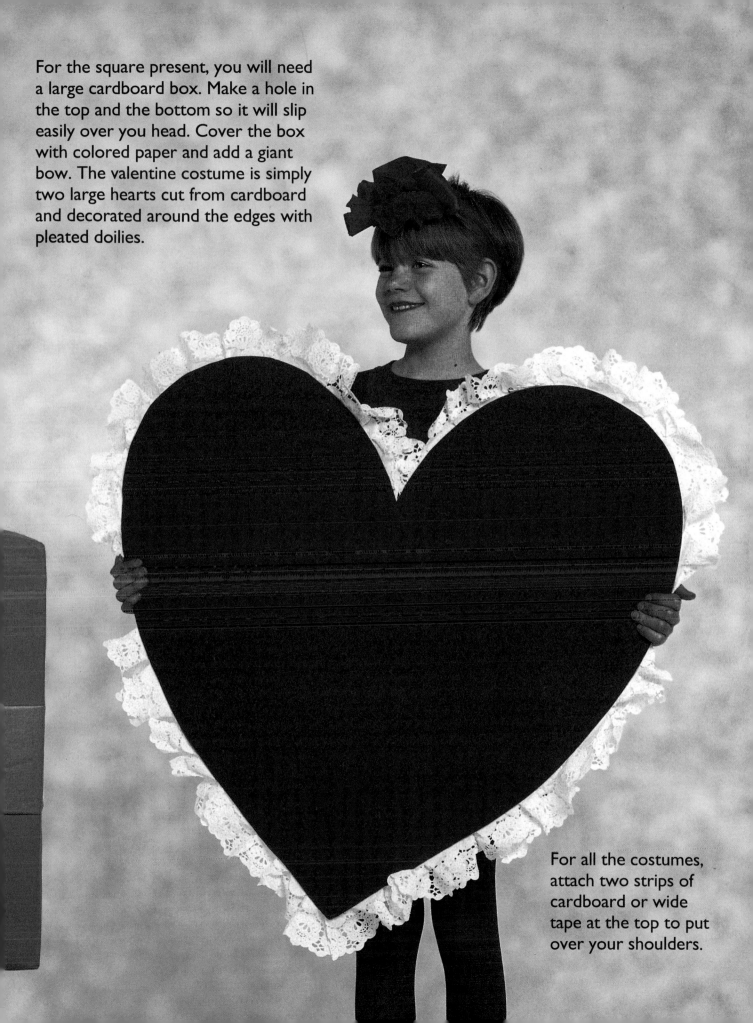

For the square present, you will need a large cardboard box. Make a hole in the top and the bottom so it will slip easily over you head. Cover the box with colored paper and add a giant bow. The valentine costume is simply two large hearts cut from cardboard and decorated around the edges with pleated doilies.

For all the costumes, attach two strips of cardboard or wide tape at the top to put over your shoulders.

Don't forget your hands and feet when you are planning your costume! You can use fabric paints to decorate canvas shoes and replace laces with ribbons. Look at the trim pages at the beginning of the book and add pompons, fringe, and bows to gloves and shoes. Or you could paint your feet and hands with body paint.

Tropical

These costumes are best for sunny days. We made the grass skirt by sandwiching pieces of twine between two layers of strong tape. The top is a piece of flowered material knotted at the front.

You can knot sarongs — made from a rectangle of fabric — in all sorts of ways. Try experimenting in front of a mirror. Look at the instructions for making flowers on page 6.

Here are some hats that are quick to put together for a party. The exotic carnival hat is simply a scarf tied in a big knot with plastic fruit attached. The Indian headdress is made from paper, and the chef's hat is white paper pleated and taped on to a circle of white cardboard. The pirate is wearing a scarf tied at the back.

We used the same basic shape for all of these hats. First, measure your head using a piece of string. Cut a large circle for the brim from a piece of cardboard. Cut a circle in the middle slightly smaller than your head measurement. Make slits around the inner circle and bend the pieces up. Make the top of the hat from a circle of cardboard in the same way. Tape or glue the top and brim to a wide band of cardboard that is bent into a circle.

INDEX